D0667183

PRAYERS
for
GIRLFRIENDS
and SISTERS
and ME

PRAYERS
for
GIRLFRIENDS
and SISTERS
and ME

EVELYN BENCE

VINE BOOKS
SERVANT PUBLICATIONS
ANN ARBOR, MICHIGAN

Vine Books is an imprint of Servant Publications especially designed to serve evangelical Christians.

All Scripture quotations, unless indicated, are taken from the HOLY BIBLE, NEW INTERNATIONAL VERSION. © 1973, 1978, 1984 by International Bible Society. Used by permission of Zondervan Publishing House. All rights reserved.

Published by Servant Publications
P.O. Box 8617
Ann Arbor, Michigan 48107

Cover photograph: © Stephan Lowe/Westlight. Used by permission.
Interior decorations from illustrations by Joanne E. Klein © 1982, 1983, 1984. Used by permission.

99 00 01 02 10 9 8 7 6 5 4 3 2 1

Printed in the United States of America
ISBN 1-56955-118-9

LIBRARY OF CONGRESS CATALOGING-IN-PUBLICATION DATA

Bence, Evelyn, 1952-
Prayers for girlfriends and sisters and me / Evelyn Bence.
    p.   cm.
Includes index.
ISBN 1-56955-118-9 (alk. paper)
1. Christian women—Prayer-books and devotions—English.   I. Title
BV4844.B395   1999
242'.843—dc21   98-53805
                                                     CIP

DEDICATION

For Suzanne,
my most enduring, endearing friend.

For my four older sisters,
Rachel, Priscilla, Norma, and Alice,
who greeted me as I entered this world.
May we welcome one another when we
cross over to the next.

CONTENTS

ACKNOWLEDGMENTS

Thank you to all the girlfriends who've laughed and cried with me for a season.

Thanks especially to Debra Wells and my sister Priscilla, for their early reading of and comments on this manuscript. To Marilyn Moore for spurring on me when I was ready to shut down. To Servant editor Bert Ghezzi for "running with it." To Kathy Deering, Diane Bareis, and the entire team at Servant for their enthusiasm and dedicated work.

INTRODUCTION

We are bartering the priceless boon, if we are looking on friendship merely as a luxury, and not as a spiritual opportunity.

HUGH BLACK, *Friendship*, 1898

To write this book I have combed my memory and imagination. Remembering a line of conversation. Recalling an event. Projecting myself into a scenario. Pulling up an emotion. I placed myself in a setting with a friend or sister, asked "what if?" and turned the situation, real or imagined, God-ward.

What would I—what might you—pray for? For a girlfriend, a sister, oneself?

At turning points: when a friend meets the man;

marries him; buys a house; has a child; celebrates a milestone; loses a child, spouse, or parent; or moves away.

At reflective moments of gratitude: for an afternoon out, a listening ear, a long loyalty, a thoughtful gift.

At relational aggravations: guidance to walk through a misunderstanding, courage to make an apology, grace to bless rather than blame.

At opportunities for spiritual growth: What would God want me to do? What would draw us closer to God? What would lead us to and along paths of righteousness?

Most of the prayers speak to women of any age, but some address concerns specific to a particular season of life. Prayers written in the voice of a young woman appear early in the book. As the book progresses, the voice ages, the concerns become those of middle-aged and then older women. As you can see in the table of contents, many of the prayer titles reveal prayer topics, but for further clarity I include a topical index.

❦❦❦

I see several ways one might use this book.

A gift book. At first I set out to write a gift book. A symbol of friendship and appreciation, blessing and goodwill. *Dear Friend-Sister, these prayers of grace are my prayers for you.* The recipient would dip into the prayers at applicable occasions, appropriate seasons, to turn her heart toward God, to remember the kind regards of the friend who gave the gift.

A reflective book about sisterhood. But as I wrote the prayers, I saw that they were themselves stories and parables about friendship. A week before I finished the manuscript, I asked a friend if she would read a bit of the printout. Not the whole thing. Just a smattering. I think I said, "Quit when it's not fun anymore," not convinced that anyone would enjoy reading prayer upon prayer upon prayer. But she stayed and stayed until she'd read every last one—some with laughter, some through tears. "This is more than a gift book," she said. "It's a story that's teaching me what 'being supportive' means." What friendship is. What sisterhood entails. "I wanted to keep reading," to find out where the thread was leading.

A devotional aid. After reading maybe twenty of the prayers, a woman considerably younger than I said she wanted to use the book as a devotional aid, reading one prayer a day for four months as a way to focus her prayer and connect her to friends and family members—whomever the prayer suited, toward whomever the Holy Spirit directed her attention.

In the end these prayers are not just for girlfriends and sisters, but also for me.

For all of us joined as one in the household of faith, called to be saints:

> The Lord bless you
>   and keep you;
> the Lord make his face shine upon you
>   and be gracious to you;
> the Lord turn his face toward you
>   and give you peace.

NUMBERS 6:24-26

DELIVER HER FLOWERS

God, I pray: For no special reason, today deliver her a bouquet of flowers. Not the too-perfect silken wonders. But the country kind that hide the nectar and give the bees a workout. A little yellow for laughter, a bit of red for passion, a bunch of white Queen Anne's lace to keep her good. And don't forget the greens: complementary reminders of growth—how far she's come, under your sunshine and with your showers of mercy.

I might deliver wildflowers myself. (I'll do that next Friday. Or maybe, rather, a single garden rose.) But for now, I put this request in your hands: Send her flowers today. No clear who's-it-from gift card attached. An unforgettable bouquet of flowers.

SISTERS *and* ME

THAT DOGGIE IN THE WINDOW

It's lunchtime. In the middle of a workday. We're walking down the street and stop at a pet shop window displaying furry puppies falling all over one another.

That's all it took. Next thing I know, she's crying. After a while she offers an explanation: "I didn't realize how very unhappy I am." In this job. In this glass, concrete, and steel city. With this life she's made for herself.

God, that was amazing—your using a bit of squirming puppy flesh to send her a message that she wouldn't have heard if I'd tried to tell her in clear language. Now that she's named her dissatisfaction, nudge her to a smile, whether it's discovering contentment here in this city, or moving out to where there are open green fields.

MR. RIGHT, MR. WRONG

God, he seemed so perfect for her, or so she thought. As if he might have been the pinnacle of your creation: pure gold molded from day one, explicitly, exclusively for her. And now he's gone and dumped her. Walked away without looking back. Isn't that proving his mettle? As in, what a jerk.

There's no convincing her that he never was good enough for her. She's not ready to hear it from me, because she still wants to believe in her idol. So—maybe you, in your good time, could turn her attention away from this clay specimen and toward one who's made to match her sterling.

STAND BY ME

God, I'm confused and unsettled, and I need some direction. Bibles and books might give guidance, but what I'd really like is a phone call, better yet, a real-cup-of-coffee conversation with my friend, who knows how to ask the right questions. Clear out the brush. Go for clarity.

Why can't I pick up the phone and call her? What's my problem? Maybe I don't really want clarity. Clarity will call for action. And it's easier to stay settled than to take a step forward. Confused and unsettled—at least I know the territory and how it feels. Taking a risk and stepping out—it feels scary. As does calling my girlfriend. Right now I can't do what I want to do—call her.

So God, in the meantime, I'll talk to you.

SHE'S ENGAGED

She called me in the middle of the night—OK, it was only 1:00 A.M., but so it seemed—to tell me she had said yes, she would marry him. Thank you, thank you for jolting me out of the cobwebs of sleep, giving me the presence of mind to rejoice with her *right then,* when she needed to share her joy.

Now, in the next months, as she's planning a party, packing to move, holding down a job, and getting a glimpse of what "till death us do part" with one man might mean, help her to hold on to the joy and, while rejoicing, let me get my sleep.

WHO'S TO BLESS, WHO'S TO BLAME?

God, today she and I made an agreement to try to give each other perspective when it comes to taking responsibility for the right stuff. Neither of us can find a healthy balance. One of us is always blaming "anyone else but me" for her own missteps. (Yes, even Adam knew how to play this game.) And the other is always blaming herself for the very existence of every piece of dust in the house. (Well, maybe not, but you get my drift.)

God, here I bring you into this agreement: Please open our eyes so we can see things as they really are. Help us to take reasonable responsibility. Help us to be gentle with others—and ourselves. Help us to be fair with ourselves—and others.

Help us to be a little less concerned with "who's to blame?" And a lot more concerned with "who's to bless?" And how?

WEDDING EMOTION

What was that about? This afternoon, in the middle of her wedding ceremony—"With this ring [or was it 'wing'?], I thee wed,"—she lost it, utterly lost it. It may have started with a nervous giggle, but quickly it exploded. The cork blew out of the champagne bottle. Convulsive laughter or tears? It was impossible to tell which. The guests snickered at first and then, as the outburst continued, grew solemnly silent, wondering what this might mean.

Was it pure joy? Was it a symptom of exhaustion? Or maybe fear? Did she feel as if she were jumping off a cliff, with no net to catch her?

Was this the happiest day of her life—or the day she will someday rue?

God, you know her vulnerable heart, how much she loves him, and how much she's giving him. A small ring is such an inadequate symbol. Bless them. Protect her. May she always be assured that this match was no mistake.

And, more immediately—this may be asking too much—but let her get some serious sleep tonight, so she doesn't ruin tomorrow.

MUSEUM AFTERNOON

I'm not sure I understand how two hours in an art museum
with a friend—pushing a stroller, even—can open up one's
closed-in world. We rehash our old themes—loves, labors,
losses—and the art puts them in perspective. Our here-and-
now is connected to the there-and-then. Light breaking in.
Water breaking over. Sweat breaking out.

God, Scripture says you have put eternity in our hearts.
Help us enlarge the frame in which we see our lives.

NEW FRIEND:
WITH THE GREATEST OF EASE

God, she approaches life as if she were a daring young thing on a flying trapeze. Meaning she makes it all look so very easy. Never a badly timed move. Never a miss. Never an effort. On a more pedestrian note, never a jumbled sentence out of her mouth. Never a bad hair day.

For me life is more like a movie set. "Take 1" didn't work, so let's try "take 2" and maybe "take 3." If I were a trapeze artist, I'd be tearing holes in the net.

I like her (I think she can teach me something about poise and control), and yet I envy her. Forgive me that envy. Give me a chance to get to know her better, to learn from her, and maybe, who knows, even to teach her something about falling headlong into grace.

SISTERS *and* ME

TAKE AND READ

I bought her a copy of a book that touched me deeply, wanting to share the ah-yes that resonated through my being, the rush of the words that brightened my whole world. Too often I asked if she'd read it yet, opened it even.

It's right there on my nightstand…. I've been so busy.

Finally, she read a few pages—but only to get me off her back.

It's time for me to lay off. She's not going to finish it. She's not going to get to the good stuff. The words that struck me with such force lie there in wait, in the dark, pressed between pages that may never be opened. Or maybe they'll be opened on the other side of a table where secondhand (though never used) books are sold.

God, I can't make her read the book that changed my outlook on life. Even if she were to read it, I can't make her "get it" just as I did—the exact nuances. This disappoints me, frustrates me. I want her to open it, mark it, digest it, savor it. Catch the vision.

Can you nudge her, please? Or—maybe it's time I realized: The words were a grace to me, not meant for her. Drop it.

WEDDING BELL BLUES

The intimacy of sisters is lost or transformed when one marries.

LOUISE BERNIKOW, *Among Women*

We used to talk about everything. We needed each other. *We*. It meant *her* and *me*. Do you remember?

She doesn't seem to, now that she's landed *him*. He gets her laughter. Her chatter. Even her tears. She leans away from me and toward him. She's not accessible anymore. She doesn't listen to me. Not that I'm doing much talking; she doesn't notice I've grown quiet.

I guess I feel abandoned. Maybe jealous of their *we,* which excludes me. It doesn't feel fair, after all our years together, sharing the same bathroom mirror.

I'm not sure there's anything I can or should do about this. But it hurts.

Lord, my sister is my best friend. I don't want to lose her. I pray you will help us find a way to transform our relationship. When the honeymoon is over, turn a bit of her laughter back toward me. In the meantime, let me let her go, with grace, so I'll be ready to welcome a new *we.*

SISTERS *and* ME

God, at a bargain basement, in a frantic rush just to "get it done," I bought her the most inappropriate present, a tacky bauble, totally tasteless. I knew it wasn't right, but I wrapped it anyway, as quickly as possible, wanting to get it out of my sight, the deed done.

It sits here, packaged well but silently condemning my efforts. Sending her a card would be better. Or cooking her a meal. Even baking cookies cut from a Pillsbury roll.

Lord, I hear you, telling me I need to take two steps back—OK, three steps—start over, slow down, give the people in my life some attention befitting their being. Send the bauble to Goodwill. (Eventually it will find a home.) Let us—you and me—wrap and ribbon this friendship with delight.

HOUSE BLESSING

Bless this house as she makes it hers:
painting particular colors,
planting exotic flowers.
Post angels on its lot lines,
guarding the good, holding evil at bay.
May hungry souls be fed within these walls
and thirsty hearts revived.
Soften the losses grieved here,
and stretch the joyful days.
Like incense in the air,
fill this space—her place—
with the sweet fragrance of your presence.
Bless this house, O God. Bless her home.

GRANT HER A SAFE DELIVERY

Any day now her first child may be released from the nest deep within the rock. But not without a crisis that will crack Gibraltar. Is she ready for this? She thinks so. With the naiveté of youth she believes the spin: Just get the breathing right and it all works naturally. No sweat.

I wish.

I hope.

God, grant her a safe delivery. Protect her baby on this, its breakthrough journey. Give my friend courage and fortitude when push comes to shove. Be right there with her, wiping the sweat dripping off her brow.

WINTER WONDER

Lord, it's as if she's shut off the heat in a room of her heart. It's cold outside, and the chill is seeping in, bringing the temperature down, down, until I'm afraid the water might freeze, the pipes break. Let her allow us in—you and me—and just give us permission to turn up the thermostat if she can't reach for it herself.

SPARE US

God, yesterday I read an Ethiopian proverb: "A close friend can become a close enemy."

Ah, impossible, I say. But the line stays in my head, sets me on edge.

Spare us, please spare us, from such a twisted fate.

SISTERS *and* ME

37

USER-FRIENDLY?

A women's magazine lays out pretty pictures of cozy—or maybe cluttered—rooms "where friendships flourish." I browse and then mentally inventory my ground floor: Is the kitchen inviting? The living room conducive? The dining room agreeable? God, should I refurbish the house? Make the environment more friend-friendly?

I listen for an answer, and my heart hears *stop, rest, breathe.*

My friends are comfortable here, with me, surrounded by these furnishings, imperfect as they are.

Fluff the pillows. Run the vacuum. Buy a flower. Let it be.

GONNA TAKE AN
INDEPENDENT JOURNEY

She called to tell me her daughter's first sentence.

Yes, what was it?

"Wanna go outside." Sitting on the inside of a window, she wanted to be on the other side, beyond the confines of enclosure. A simple, straightforward request. But now, a few hours later, the sentence feels cosmically significant. *Wanna get out of here.* It's the universal cry of birth, of youth, and, who knows, maybe of an old soul ready to die.

God, bless my friend's toddler. At every turn give her a healthy, life-affirming (age-appropriate!) "wanna go." And my friend—give her an unrelenting desire to coach this independence marathon. Help mamma keep her wanna.

GET A LIFE, PLEASE

Seldom set foot in your neighbor's house —
too much of you, and he will hate you.

PROVERBS 25:17

This verse is so … blunt.

Why did I highlight it this morning as I was perusing the proverbs?

Because recently my friend is so … present. As in get a life. Please.

She feels free to stroll right in, sit right down, let her mouth run on. This may work for TV shows, where rooms have only three walls. But in real quarters?

God, I know what it feels like, wanting to be anyplace else but home, when home is alone. Wanting to eat in anyone else's kitchen. Watch anyone else's TV. And I want her to feel welcome.

But my heart wants its retreat, and so I ask for discernment and tact, lest I be too … blunt.

And for her: I pray that you will enlarge her circle of friends and interests, her avenues of service, so she and I can hold fast a friendship that outruns a sitcom.

SHARE THE STUFF

I don't know what came over me. I went to the farmer's market and bought all this food and spent all morning peeling and chopping and saucing as if a threshing crew were coming to dinner.

About noon it hit me: So what am I going to do with this stuff? (Not quite Babette's feast but fair enough.)

Call a friend. Or call five before I find one who says, "Sure, over here there's nothing in the house to eat. Coming by."

God, thank you, for a whim—impulsive, but not foolish—that turned into an opportunity to pick up the phone and invite friends into my life, to share the fresh fruit of your fields cooked mighty fine by these, my tender hands.

SISTERS *and* ME

THE DREAM MEANS ...?

Twice in the last few months I've dreamed a colleague was distressed, in trouble. The details have dimmed, but for sure both times the setting was at home, not at the office—the milieu we share. God, I don't know much about her personal life, except that her husband is out of work, which itself is a hint she needs some help. Were the dreams a spur for me to ask her to lunch? Bake her a pie? Smile at her? Pray for her?

God, show me how to lighten her load. And you, please rally your forces to sustain her. Awaken other sleepers, dozing around the campfire.

LOST RING

She's called in a panic, trying to control her emotion.

What's wrong?

"I've lost my wedding ring."

How?

It was a garbled gardening story of leaves, rakes, mulch, garbage. But the ring is gone, and unlikely to be found.

Of course the gold isn't the issue. The ring is wound with such symbolism…. So why wouldn't its loss be, too?

God, assure her that it isn't necessarily so. Omens may portend disasters in Shakespeare, but here in real life they don't need to bode the future, which is in your good hands. Not subject to the slip of a ring from a finger.

STANDARDS OF PERFORMANCE

She's so successful at what she does, and yet she lives in fear that someday she's going to be "found out," found wanting. Someday her colleagues are going to discover that she's not as competent and confident as they think she is. *Success is for the perfect. I'm not perfect. Therefore I'm not successful, it just looks as if I am.* And this line of reasoning drives her to work longer and harder, and look better—as if by effort she could someday build herself an impenetrable tower of perfection. And prove herself worthy of praise.

I lay this scenario out as if she alone were so driven, when we both know the relentless mercilessness of perfectionism.

God, allow us together to work toward a better perspective of ourselves and our pursuits. We are mortal humans, not superwomen. If our standard of performance is perfection, of course we'll fall short. There's no getting around our limitations. But in and through our weakness, you are our sustaining strength.

THE LETDOWN OF A LIFETIME

God, she's heading for a fall, as in the Niagara. The letdown of a lifetime.

Yes, life is hard. She's learned that long ago. But this…

Please.

Can you—will you—throw her a lifeline to hold her back?

And if not, cushion her from the rocks?

And if not, spare her vital parts?

Please.

God, she feels she let you down because she lost control. This isn't about lust or gluttony or anger, but childbirth. When push didn't shove, she crossed a threshold: the pain more than she could bear. Her body broke her spirit and her prayer for strength and mercy. The panic cut her loose.

Now, her baby a healthy toddler, she still regrets her frantic breathing, faithless curses, her hellish screams.

"Why couldn't I hold on? Where was my steadfast faith?" she asks. Underneath the verbalized question I hear, *Where was my God? Where was God's gift of faith? Why was God absent to me in my need?*

Help her to resist her accusing enemy and look to you with faith—for faith—here and now. Stamp her spirit with this honest Gospel prayer: "Lord, I believe. Help my unbelief" (see Mk 9:24).

"If we are faithless, [Christ] will remain faithful, for he cannot disown himself" (2 Tm 2:13).

THE MOM WHO IS THERE

In a school essay her son called her an "invisible servant." The one who got up early, went to bed late, to keep the family functioning. Her hands—busy cooking, cleaning, combing. Her mind—balancing budgets and schedules. Her presence—resolving conflicts, calming fears.

She could receive the phrase as a compliment, not feeling the need to be the brightest star in the sky.

God, she doesn't always feel affirmed in her behind-the-scenes role. On her behalf, I thank you for this silent but tangible tribute that she can tuck away in her chest of treasures. Give her other signs that she is worth more than rubies to her family and to you.

REFORM HER WAYS

God, I wish she could see herself. She is fussing at her husband as if he were a child. It's not working. He's not reforming his ways.

She's not winning his heart. She's weaning his affections.

Give her the courage—yes, courage—to try a new tack.

WEEPING FOR HER CHILDREN

Lord, how could you let this happen? Her baby is dead. The child for whom she's been dreaming and planning—breathless, still as stone.

Whatever am I supposed to say to her? Whatever are you doing—toying with her dreams? Allowing life to take hold and then slip away so prematurely? What defense of you am I supposed to come up with? Is this what's called the awful grace of God?

Your daughter is weeping and will not be comforted. "Answer me quickly, O Lord; ... Do not hide your face" (Ps 143:7).

HOW DOES SHE DO THE SPLIT?

This woman is two different people—depending on whom she's with. It's not a matter of hypocrisy; it's a matter of perceived competency. Get her in a blue suit and sensible pumps, head her toward the office, and she's walking with confidence, Ms. Management, speaking authority. Put her in close proximity to her "family of origin" and watch her fall like a marionette cut loose.

God, I pray you will bring her to a middle ground. At work: May she give herself permission to be not goddess, but fallible human. With family: May she give herself permission to be not child, but grown woman.

A MOVING PRAYER

She's moving away. Not across town, across the continent. And not because her heart says go, but because her husband has this career that calls him. He can't throw it away. He shouldn't, they agree, but where does that leave her? Her house on the market; her yard sale in the classifieds. Her job posted; her circle broken.

It seems harder for her than for him. She's rooted herself here, in this place, these relationships, and has no hopeful vision for opportunities on the other side of the country.

God, be with her through this transition. As she emotionally pulls away. As she eventually drives away. Replant her in rich, ready soil, by streams of living water.

And another thing: Her move leaves a hole in my own life. Be here with me, even as you go with her. I pray this with confidence, knowing you are the God who resides on both sides of the Rocky divide.

THEY WANT A BIOPSY

"They found this lump. They want this biopsy." She was trying to remain calm, just relaying the news of the week, as if this were about a dental filling. But then she never would have told me about a Novacaine.

I wanted to say, "It'll be OK," meaning it won't be cancer. But how do I know what the doctors don't?

I nearly said, "Don't worry." But I remembered that it's not my body's bump.

So I said I would pray that it would be OK and I would pray that she would not worry. And I pray still. God, hear.

P.S. Delayed Praise
This time the tests were clear. God, we thank you for this blessing.

But it reminds me that not every biopsy reads benign. Not even for the young. Not especially for the old. Eventually disease and decay win. Like moths and rust. Lord, please delay the call until we're ready. Is anyone ever?

THE GIFT AND ITS PACKAGE

She sent me a gift package that is too nice—worth too much. I love it. It perfectly suits my taste, but it makes me a bit uncomfortable. As if I should reciprocate in kind ...

Lord, don't let me get started on that route. If the gift was meant to manipulate or oblige, then the spiral needs to be broken. If it was simply a thoughtful gesture, then allow me to receive it graciously, with appreciation.

Teach me a bit more about the meaning of gifts.

Receiving them. Gratefully, without trying to figure how much I owe to keep us even.

Giving them. Freely, without strings attached.

"Freely you have received, freely give" (Mt 10:8b).

WHERE'S MY MIRACLE?

She meant it so sincerely: "I just thank God for my miracle." The big one. The event for which she'd be grateful to her dying day.

I smiled. And gulped. And, I'm ashamed to admit, wondered why I'd never gotten mine.

"Rejoice with those who rejoice," wrote Paul, surely knowing that it's easier to weep with those who weep.

Help me to rejoice with her. Help me overlook her insensitivity to my oversensitivity.

And the miracle. I'm waiting, God, for my turn.

SPECIAL INTENTION

The call of the Sabbath day to cease our work and striving and productivity gives us time for such inefficient things as … enjoying one another's company, writing letters or making phone calls … spending extra time in prayer for them or making gifts.

MARVA DAWN, *Keeping the Sabbath Wholly*

Lord, you meant for us to set aside one day a week. I've lost that vision, but today I lay out a new resolution: to reclaim the Sabbath for relationship, first with you and then with family and friends.

I start with this prayer of intent and ask for your help to keep the calendar column clear of my standard efficiency demands. Give me time. No. That's already a given. Give me the desire to keep this focus and the focus to keep this desire.

GO FOR THE FLOW

God, she has such a knack for getting me unstuck.

Sometimes it's a writing project. I can't get to the next paragraph, to say nothing of the next page. My train of thought has stalled and I'm starting to panic—(should I give up and go for "delete" or maybe "implode"?)—and a coffee conversation with her will pull me out and over.

Sometimes it's a spiritual nudge, back to the fountain when I'm parked and parched in the wilderness.

I thank you and her for this refreshment.

Actually, maybe it's time to call for a break. Brew us a pot. Go for the flow.

GRADUATION MEDITATION

To march or not to march, that is her question, though I
think she knew her answer before she raised the issue in conversation. She's worked so hard, and so long, and wants
some sure-handed Robed One to grab her palm (left over
right) and present her a ticket to where she wants to be.

God, she's earned this diploma and deserves the respect
due a cap and fancy gown. For her, might you roll out a
Kodak kind of day? Then, to make the picture perfect, as we
praise her, may she thank you, God of all possibility, for her
ability, for giving her this opportunity.

SISTERS *and* ME

SHE DIDN'T MEAN TO OFFEND ME, BUT OUCH!

God, why are relationships so complicated? She couldn't possibly have meant what I *heard* her say this morning. I have no idea what she thought she was doing. I'm quite positive she didn't intend to hurt me—but she did.

What I know in my head and what I feel in my heart are not the same thing.

Now, Lord, I'm not sure what I should do. What does responsible friendship require? Do I "go for honesty" and name the pain—"speak the truth in love"? Or do I cover it with grace and move on?

I ask you for discernment. For now, as I go to bed, I lay aside the perceived offense, trusting that tomorrow morning it will have shrunk like a balloon the day after a party.

And if not … well, we'll talk in the morning. Good night.

SOME KIND OF WONDERFUL

They've been married a decade, and when she laughs he still looks at her like Adam awake from surgery, amazed at the wonder standing before him.

God, I tell her to thank you every morning for this fine specimen of a man, sharing her bed and board.

She smiles and says, "I do."

SAFE AND SECURE?

"How can I go to sleep tonight, worried some burglar might be picking the lock?"

A thief broke into her place and stole more than a computer, a piece of property. That bandit stole her peace of mind, her rhythm of respect.

We all like to think we are safe and secure behind the walls we build or buy and choose to call home. And then the boundaries are violated, and we suddenly see the fragile nature of our frame: that we are dust and live in houses made of straw.

God, in the aftermath of this crime, first and foremost, calm her fear.

In good time allow her to secure the order of her daily routine.

And for all time help her see where her real surety lies— in you, her refuge, her fortress; her dock, her door.

SURVIVORS OF THE FIERY TRIAL

> Nothing can match the treasure of common memories of trials endured together.
>
> ANTOINE DE SAINT-EXUPÉRY

We're survivors, she and I. Not that we thought so at the time, walking through the fiery ordeal—our whole department laid off. That meant us. Suddenly reaching for parachutes. Rewriting résumés. Repackaging our lives.

God, thank you, not so much for the trial itself, but for the bond it welded between us. Survivors with similar stories and scars, and sometimes now even smiles.

SISTERS *and* ME

ALMOST—NOT QUITE—HEAVEN

She's deliriously happy. God, please give her a prolonged season of delight. Even heighten her senses till she thinks she's standing in the foyer of heaven, catching the celestial, sensual overflow.

But I pause to pray for her one curious line buried in *The Book of Common Prayer:* Lord, in your love, "shield the joyous." I hardly understand it, and yet I sense the elated need a special protection. She suddenly seems as vulnerable as a young child lured by the Pied Piper.

Shield her today. Protect her from friend or foe who might inadvertently or intentionally take advantage of her in her euphoria. Keep her from making foolish mistakes she'll soon regret.

Shield her tomorrow or next week or next year, when she wakes up and finds herself here on this grave earth. Protect her again, from enemies of the spirit that might convince her that she never knew the joy or that she's lost it forever or that it's meant for every day of the year.

Shield her in her joy. Shield her in its wake.

IS THIS MY PROBLEM?

God, a bit of competition is leaking into this friendship, and I don't get it. I might understand it better if we were professional colleagues vying for a corner office. But it's on the domestic front. Who lays out a better meal? Who gives a more festive party?

Did I innocently start this because I like to cook and "fuss" for guests? Because I get some satisfaction in presenting my well-planned meals as gifts? Maybe, as I eventually sensed that my spinach-stuffed meat loaf and green bean supreme and strawberry trifle (not exactly caviar and baked Alaska) were intimidating her. I got hints of her entertaining me being a full-course event, an all-day chore.

God, is this my problem? Does my "satisfaction" come across as "snobbery"?

Or is it hers? Is her insecurity eating away at our relationship?

For the sake of friendship, do I need to serve tuna salad and spaghetti from a jar?

BE GENTLE

She takes such pride in her children, yes, but mostly in her mothering. Being present and attentive. Providing stimulation and applause. Building foundations, setting boundaries.

She has never said it in so many words, but I sense she has a theory: If I love my children enough, I can protect them from harm.

God, I wish it were so. Didn't your chosen Mary, the most blessed mother, wish it were so …?

This is a hard lesson, learning the limits of mother-love. For reasons I don't understand, your teaching methods on this point are not always tender and gentle.

With my dear friend, your dear daughter, I pray that you might be gentle, Lord. Please be gentle.

SISTERS *and* ME

MAKE ME A GOOD LISTENER

We should always have in our heads one free and open corner
where we can give place, or lodging as they pass, to the ideas of our
friends. It really becomes unbearable to converse with men whose
brains are divided into well-filled pigeonholes, where nothing can
enter from outside.

JOSEPH JOUBERT

God, make me a better listener. Not with an agenda. (How
can I refute this argument? What's wrong with this picture?
How can I top this story?) But with an open mind. Enjoying the company. Relaying respect. Looking for new wonders of your grace.

Then give me discernment to know how to respond to
what I've heard, to know which ideas I should retain or
digest, and which should just pass on through.

RISK MANAGEMENT

"This is not a game," she admitted, first to herself and then to me. This "dance" she's started with this man who has wound himself around her heart.

Oh, I remember the day I was able to say that very sentence myself. *This relationship is not a game. Not anymore. Or at least it shouldn't be. Someone could get hurt. Someone. Maybe me. Maybe him. Maybe both of us—though differently.*

God, I think it's you who brought me—and now my friend—to the point where we can see the reality of risk. *Potential heartbreak ahead.* And then assess our positions. *Is it time to step back? Or time to stay the course, go for broke?*

God, give her guidance as she tries to manage the risk.

ANTICIPATION

"Suppose this book 'takes off' and Oprah calls? What do I do? What will I say?"

OK, so the "suppose" was a bit premature. I didn't have a manuscript. Or a publisher. I'm not sure the question deserved an answer, but she landed a quip: "First you'll throw up...."

Months later, she was the one to propose the long shot: "What if he wants to marry me? Would I have to move? Where would we live?"

OK, so the "what if" was a bit premature. She hadn't actually met him. (No. I didn't toss back her line, "First you'll...".)

Sometimes it's just a game, like chess, to lay out the if and if and if. Forget the game: The mental exercise *can* prevent unnecessary defeat, but sometimes it's a worry—or a hope—run wild. A wait too painful to endure.

God, keep us from wasting energy anticipating the best or dreading the worst, so we can focus on writing the book, meeting the man—the next step, here at hand.

SISTERS *and* ME

God, for this I thank her and you: If she knows things are falling apart over here, she rarely offers a vague "let me know if there's anything I can do." If she senses that listening isn't enough, she starts with something specific. "May I drive you to the airport?" "May I come by tomorrow evening and help you paint that room?" And occasionally when I'm sick, she acts without asking: "I'm bringing over Jell-O and chicken soup."

Yes, thank you, for such a friend, who names something she's willing and able to do and lays the offering in front of me. Help me to reciprocate the grace.

MORNING PRAYER

Little things mean everything.

SAMUEL JOHNSON

God, please grant her one fine day.
A cup of coffee alone with you.
A task to complete for your glory.
A ponderable thought.
A hearty laugh.
An affectionate hug.
An evensong.
A midnight prayer.

IF THOSE WHO WISH COULD PRAY

Those who always pray are necessary to those who never pray.

VICTOR HUGO

She seems angry at the God she claims doesn't exist.

She says she has no faith, and yet she occasionally asks me to pray for her, as if she had hope.

And a few times when I've said, "I'll pray for you," she's whispered thank you.

God, by your love, turn her anger into grief, her hope into faith, her thanks into praise to you, Almighty. Amen.

WE'RE ADULTS, NO?

"We're adults. We can do this." The words, directed at me, came from a twelve-year-old, a friend's daughter, helping me put out a picnic. Everything was finally ready, except for hauling the hampers and coolers down the street.

I was waiting for some promised "help"—as in guys. She was ready for work.

Bless her, her innocent admonition made me laugh, shamed me to action, renewed the lost vigor of my lost youth.

God, thank you for young friends who can hit a target without even aiming their shots.

But all too soon she and I will indeed be two adults, women standing side by side, the twenty-five years between us inconsequential to our camaraderie. Or so I pray—Lord, let it be.

SISTERS *and* ME

SHORT TAKE

Sitting in a jail cell, Martin Luther King said he had time to "pray long prayers."

For any number of reasons, long prayers are beyond me right now. So I present this short one: I'm filled with fear, feeling as if my life is teetering on the brink. God, bring me back to the center. Send an encouraging friend into my life *today*. That's all. Please. Thank you. Please.

SURGERY REQUIRED, TOO YOUNG

I realize this was her initial and raw reaction, but is a hysterectomy cause for hysteria? Would I respond the same way? Maybe. If I hadn't been expecting such drastic measures.

It's a big deal. Losing the rhythm marked by the monthly show, the reminder of the potential of life—not this time, but maybe next—and the assurance that there will be a next time. Another chance to bear. Another chance at immortality, feigned though it be.

God, let her grieve the children she might have borne. Assure her that her womb is not her heart. That the scalpel will not stop the flow of her lifeblood. That her womanhood will survive the surgeon's knife.

DISCONSOLATE

Disconsolate. It's an old-time word that wraps it up—my frame of mind when I showed up at her doorstep.

She took one look at me and said, "What's *wrong?*"

I didn't even answer but let her pull me inside.

What did she do? She wrapped me in her arms and let me cry. She listened to me stammer. Left me curled in a ball on her couch while she went to the kitchen and cooked comfort food, which she coaxed me to eat, singing an old hymn as if it were a lullaby: "Come ye disconsolate ... Come to the mercy seat ... Here bring your wounded heart ... Earth has no sorrow that heaven cannot heal."

God, thank you for the piece of heaven that fed me in this, my earthbound friend.

TRAVELER'S MERCIES

God, she needs this vacation so badly. A change of scenery. A chance to breathe deeply. But she's apprehensive about the travel. So much can go wrong.

For this trip I pray a special detail of angels keeping watch, guarding her path, guiding her safely as she heads away from home, and again as she returns, renewed and refreshed, having found comfort at every station. Mercy at every bend.

SISTERS *and* ME

OPEN WOUNDS

God, your Word says the wounds of a friend are faithful—at least when compared to the "deceitful" kisses of an enemy.

Right now I could take some kisses.

Because "the friend" is hurling gravel, smooth and small and hard. "If I weren't your friend, I wouldn't be telling you this…. You've got a problem here…. A real blind spot…."

O God. These wounds feel anything but faithful. I'm hurt and angry and distrustful. How do I know—is she a friend, or is she an enemy showing her true self?

Lord, I make three requests:

Heal my wounds.

Allow me to accept any truth contained in her hard words.

Show me whether I should trust her as a friend or love her as an enemy.

CRISIS MANAGEMENT

This crisis of hers, it's not settling quickly, and, God, to you I admit I'm feeling drained, weary in well-supporting. It's as if her crisis were becoming my crisis.

Lord, in Scripture I see what seems to be a contradiction: We are to bear one another's burdens, yet each of us is called to bear her own.

So I don't know exactly how to do this right. Show me how to be and bear, for her and with her. Teach both of us that on the most basic level, the burdens shouldn't be ours at all; we're to cast them on you, living each day by faith, knowing you already carried the ultimate burden to the grave.

WHAT ARE YOU AFRAID OF?

"I can't move ahead with it," I said.

"Why?" she asked.

I gave an answer we both knew was hooey.

"What are you afraid of?"

Ugh. Why did she have such a good aim? For honesty's sake, I tried to name the fear that held me back from stepping into a new venture. "OK, I'm afraid I might fall, fail." But suddenly naming *one* wasn't giving the complete picture. I almost whispered: "And what if I don't fail? What if I make it? Maybe I'm afraid I'll succeed. Success. It could be a burden. A responsibility. Think of the change it would bring."

Afraid to lose. Afraid to win. She smiled. I tried to.

God, thank you for her pointed question. Thank you for giving me the courage and clarity to name my fear aloud, in her presence and yours. Now help me take the next step, to make a decision based on faith and not fear.

TWO ARE BETTER THAN ONE

Occasionally she calls, primarily to ask me to pray for her. She's feeling overwhelmed and isolated and needy. (Sometimes physically sick.) And she's looking for assurance that she's on someone's mind. First mine. Then yours. Or maybe the other way around.

God, she hasn't called recently, and yet I pray for her today. Not because she's on my list of needs I'm afraid you might ignore if I didn't bring them to your attention. But because I want to join my heart with yours. For her good.

SISTERS *and* ME

KEEP IN TOUCH

Absence does not always make the heart grow fonder. It only does so, when the heart is securely fixed, and when it is a heart worth fixing. More often the other proverb is truer, that it is out of sight out of mind.

HUGH BLACK, *Friendship*

God, when I move away next month will we keep in touch?

We say we will, but we don't define the phrase. Christmas letters? Birthday calls? E-mail jokes? Occasional spontaneous chats? More deliberate visits?

God, maintaining friendships takes time and attention. It doesn't happen without some initiative, and it's so easy to get busy and preoccupied with the demands of this present moment.

PRAYERS *for*

I pray the foundation we have fixed for this friendship will be secure enough to endure the loss of a common environment. And if it's not, may we remember each other with fond thanksgiving. And Christmas greeting.

SINGLE MOTHER, MONEY MADNESS

God, she's raising these kids alone. I knew she was financially strapped, but she just told me she hasn't been to the dentist in five years. "It's me or the kids," she says. So she takes them for checkups—even got her daughter braces—but tunes out the dentist's lecture to her. And now she tunes out mine. Acts as if I'm talking to Harvey the invisible pooka.

God, am I supposed to write her a check—a Christmas present? Insist that she make an appointment while I stand and watch her dial? (Please, tell me no.)

Is the daughter having *braces*—beautiful teeth in ten years—more important than the mother having *teeth* in ten years? (Or is this idea of going to the dentist even if nothing hurts just modern hoopla?)

I'm full of questions today. I don't know my role in this relationship. It would be easiest just to forget what she told me, let her live her own life and be responsible for the way she spends what little money she has. But is easiest "best"? What does "good friend" mean? Suddenly I feel clueless. Help.

WHAT'S THIS ANGER?

God, she's becoming an angry woman, expecting offense around every corner, anticipating the negative, and then spreading it like manure one can hardly help but step in. I'm tired of watching where I walk. She complains to me about everything but me. OK, I can be thankful for small graces—that she doesn't take me on. (Though sometimes I wonder what she is saying to whom about me, wretch that she might perceive me to be.)

She hasn't always been this way. What set it off? What will reverse the pattern, lighten her spirit? And what's my role? I don't want to turn a deaf ear, but I don't want her to drag me down. It's no place I care to be, wallowing in the muck.

CHRONIC PAIN

She's trying so hard to maintain a life-as-normal stance and routine. She gets up every morning and tells herself that she has a choice: to dwell on the negative or go for the positive. She tries not to talk about the pain, but I can see it in her eyes. And occasionally, in the middle of a sentence, she stops and stares, momentarily caught in the grip of a merciless trap, and then she coaxes herself a little room, and can finish the thought.

God, I don't understand why she is suffering so, and for months that now add up and divide down to years. She doesn't deserve this pain.

If I were a better friend I would ask you to take it from her and place it on me. But I'm not that perfect friend, so in frailty, I pray you will take her pain from her. Period. And with faith in who you are, I pray you will assure her that you have already taken it on yourself. Lord, hear my prayer.

SLOW-GROW

God, her adolescent boys are giving her a run. The manager at Roy Rogers kicked the whole family out last week. Then the boys threw a mattress out a second-story window, hoping to hit the dog. As for hitting—they can't keep their hands off each other, as if the brotherly flesh were a punching bag. Will things get rowdier before these kids reach their destined stature?

In this season, remind her of the blessing in your design that children are delivered in small sizes, with limited mobility, limited personality, limited volition. That a child grows more slowly than the eye can perceive and gains independence (can it be called maturity?) one day at a time. Slowly enough for love to hold on. Yes, it's a blessing. Allow her to thank you for the slow-grow.

CONFLICTED CONVICTION

She and I agree. We are called to travel the high road. But then we keep discovering differences in our opinions of exactly where the road runs. *You're so legalistic, uptight....* *You're so lax, lazy ... loose.*

God, we both feel we're walking in your will. But the relationship between us is pulling taut, both of us tired of feeling we need to justify ourselves in the presence of the other. (Not that we're forever talking about "our convictions"; it's just in the air.)

So I pray: Keep us both listening, first to you and then to each other. Help us both "cling to what is good" (Rom 12:9), and show us what that means.

SISTERS *and* ME

PARENTAL GUIDANCE REQUESTED

When it comes to raising her children, she's bewildered about balance.

She wants to protect them; she wants to teach them how to walk with confidence, not fear.

She wants to give them more than she was given as a girl; she wants them to know what she learned about having to "make do."

She wants to smooth their rocky road; she wants them to be resilient.

God, your Word says, "If any of you lacks wisdom, he should ask God, who gives generously to all without finding fault" (Jas 1:5). So on her behalf, I pray: Now and for the next ten (make that thirty) years, your parental guidance is requested. Grant her wisdom. Make the rough places plain.

CLAIM THE BLAME

We cannot break off the threads of the web, and then, when the mood is on us, continue it as though nothing had happened. If such a breakage has occurred, we must go back and patiently join the threads together again.

HUGH BLACK, *Friendship*

I'm sorry. What I did was wrong, an utter violation of trust and friendship. It wasn't just a matter of her being overly sensitive and too easily taking offense. My saying, "I'm sorry if I offended you," isn't going to cut it. This one requires a clear, "I'm sorry. I was wrong. Will you please forgive me?"

God, it seems easier to lay this out with you (your conversational pauses are so subtle) than to pick up the phone, anticipating her pained hesitations as we work this through—or so I hope.

God, this is hard. Please grace me with the assurance of your forgiveness. Please give me courage to swallow my pride and claim the blame for this breach of trust.

God, she's starting to lie about her age to protect her career. Yes, she's in a profession where the youthful edge counts for everything and yet ...

It shouldn't be considered necessary. It shouldn't be a pressing temptation. It just shouldn't *be*. She—my utterly trustworthy friend—twisting the facts and living a fiction.

What do I do with this information? Show my disapproval? Speak no comment? Laugh as if it's no different from coloring one's hair? Cry because it's pathetic?

God, the lie may buy her a few years to strut her stuff. But it's not the answer to her problem. Help her come to grips with the realities of life and its limitations. And in your good time, ease her into a satisfying second career.

COLOR ME WELL

When you're in a low state of mind, sympathy isn't always so good for you.

ELEEN, QUOTED BY ROBERT AND JANE COLES,
Women in Crisis II

Sometimes it feels so good to feel so bad.

Yes, but sometimes my sister just won't let me stay there—playing, replaying the pitiful piece. Color me blue. Pin me a special-merit badge just for getting out of bed.

Lord, before healing a man who could not walk, you asked him if he wanted to get well. The man didn't give a straight answer. *I don't have enough help. I can't.* As if you hadn't heard those excuses, you said, "Get up!" (Jn 5:8). Pick up your pallet. Move on out. Know you can and should.

Which is sometimes what any of us needs to hear. Me today. Maybe her tomorrow.

From you. From each other.

God, color me better. Color us well.

SISTERS *and* ME

93

PREGNANT AND PANICKED

O God, she's pregnant. Again. At this age—when her mind is mostly on balancing a budget to make her daughter's college tuition payments. She says she's throwing up a lot. (It's too early for traditional nausea.) "I wish I could just vomit it away." Her husband is as wild-eyed as she.

"Don't do anything drastic," I told her, trying to sound more calm than I felt on her behalf.

God, implant in her—and her husband—a tiny seed of desire for this child she never intended to bear. And then allow that seed to grow bit by bit as the wombed one grows cell by cell. Make room in her heart and home for this child. By your grace, keep this child safe.

P.S. "I CAN'T BELIEVE THEY DID IT"
And Lord, as an extra mercy, I pray: Prepare the way for her teens to accept the news of a newcomer. Accepting "the shame"—for the joy set before them.

PRAYERS *for*

RENEW A ROMANCE

She says she's bored with her life. Bored with the scenery that never changes, like Moses and Miriam treading the wilderness. And what a desert it is: There's the commute, the domestic routine, the husband. She pauses. That utterly intimate noun hangs in the air between us.

Later she mentions she's run into an old flame. Wouldn't you know it, as charming as paradise.

"Be careful," I say.

"What do you mean?"

"You've got a marriage to work on."

God, help her turn her attention back to the man she said she would cherish till death.

And her husband—shake him up a bit. Renew a romance. Show him how easy it is to walk a wife to the land of promise. Milk and honey.

WRITE HER ANOTHER SONG

She's landed an interview for a job—one she really wants. I can understand her excitement and her anxiety. But she's building this up as if it were potentially the last day of the rest of her life. She's convinced that her entire future hinges on one hour of one day. *If I get this job, every piece of my profession will fall into place. If I don't get this job, bring out Barbra Streisand: "No more songs for me."*

God, may she walk into that room in top form: warm smile, quick, competent answers, insightful questions. Confident but not cocky. Pump her enough adrenaline to polish her performance, not enough to color it.

But I pray also you will help her see that her win-lose, success-failure obsession is a lie. Her life, her star, will not fall if or because she doesn't get this job.

If this job "isn't right," send her another lead. Write her another verse. Or maybe a whole new song.

CAN THIS FACE BE SAVED?

"Let's play makeup."

This wasn't my idea, beautification being beyond my reach and play being beyond the season's imagination. But one rainy evening when I was visiting from out of town, she brought out a bag of bottles and tubes, brushes and pads. "It all begins with toner," she said with authority. And then she made me over. Concealing, highlighting, feathering. Canyons, ridges, lashes. And finally the lips, the ruby-slipper lips.

I looked in the mirror and smiled. In the guise of a game she had just given me a lesson we both knew I would never request at a cosmetics counter.

She was taking a bit of a risk, wasn't she? (I *could* have taken offense—assumed she disapproved of my poor presentation.) But we both were blessed, then and still, with laughter and grace to save this face.

God, thank you for the foundation of affection on which this friendship is laid.

SISTERS *and* ME

God, she framed her news in nouns: "Allen has left the marriage." Not personal pronouns: "He—my husband—has left me."

We hadn't talked in some time; he'd been gone for months, so the first rush of emotion had flushed through. Now she was just trying to hold on, get from today to tomorrow, maintain some modicum of normalcy for the children, for herself.

As she buries and tamps a trust, a bond, a "we," may she plant seeds that in time will sprout green and even bloom with small flowers of grace: a forget-me-not, a morning glory, a prayer plant, a bit of love-in-a-mist, a sprig of sage.

But who says the blossoms need to be small? Maybe one of the sparrows you keep your eyes on could slip in a sunflower seed, a promise of bold blessing, so that she can see your love in terms of personal pronouns: Jesus—my Love—is here with me.

SIGNIFICANT BIRTHDAY

The imminent birthday might well be—should be—cause for grand celebration of decades well lived, of wisdom well gained. But she's not seeing it that way. She's counting hairs well grayed and years well removed from youth. And who am I to fault her, knowing how I brace myself for every birthday. So … what is my prayer for her—and for me when my momentous day comes around?

I pray a day of sunshine. A spirit of celebration for life itself. A cake baked for her, not by her. And candles lit in her honor, blown out with a hopeful breath.

And, Lord, what do you think? Would you disapprove if I sent her a check, to cover the cost of getting her hair colored?

BREAK OUT

I meant to do my work today—
But a brown bird sang in the apple tree
And a butterfly flitted across the field,
And all the leaves were calling me....
So what could I do but laugh and go?

RICHARD LE GALLIENNE

God, we needed a little rebellion. Not against you or the order of the universe. Against the constraints we place around ourselves. Don't slurp the watermelon. Don't cook with real cream. Don't buy roses for your own bureau. Don't go to bed until the dishes are clean.

It's never worked before: on the same day both of us ready for a break *and* finding each other. But today she called, asked if I could get away, go out and play. I just couldn't find my practiced, *No, I'm really tied up today. Got to keep my focus here.*

Let's go. Let's do. A drive to the lake. A walk on the waterfront. Stones to skip. A jar of Bubbles to blow. An ice cream cone dipped in chocolate.

Thank you, Lord, for one fine day on which the *shoulds* stayed home while we took a hike.

WHAT A FRIEND WE HAVE IN JESUS

God, why is this getting so complicated? She thinks that I think that she thinks…. And I hear this from someone else, not from her. You'd think we were still in junior high. I'm tempted to just walk away and pretend I'm not party to any of this.

Right now, I admit I'm not much interested in doing the right thing. Or even in asking you to show me what that might mean. I'm just irritated and wanting to vent. And I can't think of anyone else I can trust.

SEE JANE MOURN SPOT

She came downstairs this morning and found her dear Spot dead on the kitchen floor. This news by e-mail, sent to her entire address book, needing us to know. Her furry fellow had been with her sixteen years, longer than her husband. Had welcomed her guests. Shared her bed. Broken her boredom. Begged her love.

God, this pet was family to her. A joy and a trust. A focus and a distraction.

And her loss is real. Reason for a pause.

So here I ask you to ease her grief. Help her lay him to rest. With my sympathy. Not a lick, not a promise, but a prayer.

PRESERVING THE JOURNEY

In my journal, I record conversations ... that have helped me spiri=
tually.... This section of my journal is a record of my memorable
human interactions.

VALERIE BELL, *She Can Laugh at the Days to Come*

Last winter I sorted through a desk drawer full of old letters,
written when we lived in separate cities and were too poor to
call often (and, of course, before the days of e-mail). The letters prompted me to page through more recent journals
written on Sunday afternoons, recounting bits of significant
conversations, long-distance by phone lines, over coffee, on
the bike path—encouragements, observations, admonitions.
"Are you sure about that?" "You're doing *what?*"

Lord, I value this record of a bit of the best (OK, and also
a bit of the worst) of this friendship. Thank you for prompt-
ing me to preserve the journey, not for the sake of my grand-
children. For the sake of my very own self.

EXPANDING GRACE

God, today, sitting in traffic, I was thinking of my friends, the old ones, the newer ones. When and how did they enter my circle? Most often one friend introduced me to another, by hosting a dinner, holding a party, organizing a picnic, giving me a phone number. God, thank you for this expanding grace, which widens my world.

Help me be more intentional about extending the networks, making the links that connect other women in to the friendship of friends and even the friendship of you.

SISTERS *and* ME

WHAT'S THE WEATHER?

It is terribly amusing how many different climates of feeling one can go through in one day.

ANNE MORROW LINDBERGH, *Bring Me a Unicorn*

She's a bit, well, moody. When she's up, she's very, very up. But then the barometer drops.

Why? Do her shoes pinch her toes? Have her hormones gone awhack? Does she need a chiropractic crack? Or—there's always that fear—is it something I said or left unsaid? Is she upset with *me*?

God, help me understand the cause of the weather patterns. Teach me patience. Protect me from paranoia.

But I pray you will in turn teach her the value, even power, of a word spoken fitly, a storm suffered gladly.

PRAYERS *for*

DEATH OF A HUSBAND

He was the love of her life, the only man to know her. Truly. Madly. Deeply.

Till death them do part. And now it does.

Forsaking all others. And now forsaken she stands by the shell of the man she always dreamed to have. Was grateful to hold.

As long as they both shall live. She cannot imagine life without him, and yet she does still move and breathe. Her flesh surviving her loss, though she might wish it otherwise.

God, comfort her in her grief. Enfold her in your arms and show her how very much you love her. Truly. Madly. Deeply.

Till death them do rejoin. And beyond that. Forevermore.

HELP HER MAKE IT
THROUGH THE NIGHT

My sister called, says she can't sleep, or when she does, she most often drifts into nightmares. It was more than a report. It was a plea for prayer or help. And she calls me because we grew up in the same bedroom, shared the same night air for so many years.

That was long ago and she is far away.

God, please: Daytime, nighttime, any other fright time, draw her toward the light and peace of your presence. Tonight, tomorrow, and the day after that, stay with her in the dark. Sit by her bed and whisper sweet somethings till she falls asleep. Then, when she starts to dream, maybe you could leave a celestial night-light on, so the Dark runs out of room.

SHE'S EATING HER HEART OUT

God, she's eating as if there's no tomorrow, as if this meal, though surely not this very bite, might be her last. (At this clip, it might be.) When I asked, she admitted she's up two dress sizes in just a year.

She said she's depressed because she's gaining weight.

I asked a more basic question: Are you gaining weight—eating—because you're depressed?

The conversation shut down.

God, what's she doing? And why? Help me to keep the conversation going. Or if she can't talk with me, let her find someone else with whom she can figure the why and find the want to get back to reason.

It may be winter, but summer's coming. Let her be here and be fit to enjoy it.

SISTERS *and* ME

THE BRIDE AND MR. NICE GUY

Her daughter is getting married. Everyone agrees he's a "nice young man." But today when no one was home at her place, my friend called to unload. The conversation boiled down to "She—daughter—shouldn't be settling for nice. She's falling for the wedding—not the man—of her dreams."

Behind my friend's words I sensed a disappointment in her own marriage: *I regret having settled for nice.... For my daughter I had wished—I still wish—for more.*

God, show the mother some way to be true to her reservations yet genuinely supportive.

As for her own marriage, give her some time to grieve the knight dream.

MENTOR MEANS ...

Last week I heard that my first boss has died. I haven't seen her in years and yet, nine-to-five, she's never far from my mind. Steering me in. (What would *she* do? How would *she* react?) And cheering me on. (You can do anything *if* you put your mind to it.) Suddenly, with her departing this realm, I feel a little frayed, maybe abandoned and betrayed—that she's gone and left me here to figure the rest of this out on my own.

God, back then I didn't realize how amazing she was, secure enough to count us as a team. (We were a team before teams were cool.) Secure enough to share her territory and trust me with her knowledge.

Thank you for giving me such a gift. Thank you for giving me the sense to honor her gift, even when I hardly understood its value.

Now give me the opportunity and the self-confidence to pass the package on to a younger woman working her way through the maze.

A fitting memorial? Maybe.

IT HAD BEEN YEARS, AND YET ...

God, I hadn't seen her in five years and yet we could spend a day together and pick right up as if we'd seen each other last week. Oh sure, over the first cup of coffee, we oohed and aahed at wallet photos. We chronicled new physical aches and pains. But soon we moved on to naming triumphs, fears, disappointments, dreams.

It may be another five or fifteen years before we see each other again. We both knew that. And yet I think we both felt confident that we would be able to reconnect—as if a year were a day.

God, through your grace, may it be.

SAYS SHE'S GOING TO TAKE A HIKE

She tells me—swears me to secrecy—that she's fallen in love with "someone else" and is making plans to leave her husband in four months, when her youngest child goes back to college in the fall.

God, I don't want to know this. It makes me feel responsible to *do* something to *fix* what's broken. Of course I can't fix it. I can tell her I disapprove; I can suggest ways to engage her husband or to disengage her new love; I can talk to her head, but I'm not sure I can get through to her heart. But then if I talk "don't" too long or loud, she's going to shut me out. (Or is this just my generation's easy excuse for not getting involved?)

So, what do I do? If someone's going to get through to her *heart*, it's going to have to be you. I ask you please to start talking, Spirit to spirit. You're free to use me. But could you also assure me that I'm not responsible for her walk?

SISTERS *and* ME

WHAT DOES A WOMAN WANT?

I called over the weekend and got right to the point: "I need some 'ttention."

"Oh, poor baby," she appropriately answered. "Let me grab a cup of coffee." And we both laughed.

God, thank you for a friend with whom I can name my need, as infantile as it may be. Maybe she's learned this from you.

HOW LONG? TOO LONG

God, her parents are coming to visit and they're staying how long? Too long. She feels she needs to put out three well-planned meals a day (though after a few days it's not clear whose plan is winning—hers or her mother's). And then her dad gets restless, looking for projects (which she's got plenty of, but he always needs a handler).

"Don't fuss."

She tries not to.

"It's just us."

She knows.

But her routine is broken. And she reverts to a daughtering role for, yes, too long.

God, give her patience with them and with herself. And grace every day of their visit, with a few minutes of laughter. Let them find little ways to honor each other, so they all remember the visit fondly, with appreciation for the attention, the time, the blessed bonds.

GIRLFRIENDS *and* SISTERS *and* ME

TELEPHONE LAUGHTER

Thank you for a good case of the giggles. We haven't talked in a year, but she called me tonight to say hello, and you would have thought we were schoolgirls. We were laughing at "do-you-remember-when?" college events that seem funny now, looking back, but as you surely know, were then moments of utmost embarrassment. The day we were walking across an intersection, and my shiny black half slip slipped off. (Did I pick it up or keep walking? I couldn't remember, though she did.) The day I dared her to pin every brooch she owned onto her blouse and walk to the dining hall for dinner. (She did, though only briefly shedding her coat.)

Silly kids we were. And blessed—then and still—to have found the pleasure of each other's company. Thank you for the find.

THE RITUALS

I can see that over the years we've established patterns. Who calls whom and when. Who drops by, for what reason. The greetings, the gestures. The pauses, applauses. I'm not sure when they set themselves in place, but they've become rituals. Expectations that emanate grace. Thank you for a friend's predictable favor. Help me not take it for granted.

AFRAID TO CRY

God, she says she's afraid to cry. Afraid she'll never stop. I assure her there's a time to mourn, and from my experience, I'd say the sooner the better. It's like a birth. You have to let go of the fetus before you can cuddle the baby. And you have to let go of the pain before you can cradle the joy.

If she lets down her guard and cries for hours or days, Lord, assure her—as you assured the psalmist—that you are the Tender of tears. You catch and measure them. Bottle and label them. Safe in your keeping. Forever. Amen.

BLESS THE GIVER AND THE GIFT

Every good and perfect gift is from above, coming down from the Father of the heavenly lights, who does not change like shifting shadows.

JAMES 1:17

God, you know how diligently she's worked to piece and quilt this covering—for love of her child, to warm his bed and please his eye. She's been stitching on this *magnum opus* for months. (Or is it years?) Her gift to her son and his bride. And last night she tied the last thread.

OK, it's not going to win first prize at the state fair, but it is a right fine piece. Her creative eye, her steady, intentional hand, her sacrifice of hours—all cause for applause, worthy of celebration.

God—Creator, Carpenter, Gift-Giver—you know about designing and crafting and presenting. Bless the quilter and the quilt. The hands that made it. The eyes that behold it. The children who hide under it.

GIVE HER A SUCCESS

God, I've had my share of humiliations, but enough successes to know that I'm good at something. You've blessed me. Approaching fifty, my friend is still floundering, hoping for a hit but mostly afraid of another strikeout. And she does have a history of, well, opportunities lost, for any number of reasons: some bad swings, no swings; foul hits, high flies; stupid steals, nasty tags.

Here's my prayer: Give her a solid base hit. On her team set someone behind her who can and will give her a chance to run to second and third. And a coach, Lord. She needs someone seasoned who can help her get it right—to risk, but not foolishly.

What? Who? Me? Oh. I don't know. I'm not sure. I might not be good at it. It might strain our relationship, try our patience. She might think I'm intruding….

God, I'm willing, I guess, to give a little coaching. But give me the right cautions, encouragements, signals. The right spirit.

And please, give her the next run home.

A GRANDMOTHER'S PRIDE
AND PREJUDICE

God, she's more excited about the birth of her grandchild than she was about the arrival of any of her own children. This time around, all gain, no pain. All pride, sheer prejudice.

Please protect her family.

The little ones, who link her to the future.

The bigger ones, who push them in prams and cuddle them in bosoms and pray for them through the night.

SISTERS *and* ME

THIS COULD BE MESSY

She and her husband are teetering on the brink of separation. She's angry and confused and telling me stuff about her husband she may wish I didn't know if they ever get back together.

Frankly, I never could figure out what she saw in him— not that I ever said anything negative, not that he seemed all *that* bad. But now I like him even less, and today I said something about him that *I* may regret if they ever get back together.

O God, this could be messy.

I pray they do get some help and decide to work things out. They have some good team potential. But if they do get back together, those words—of hers, of mine—I don't know if they'll clog the drain of our relationship and require us to use a plunger, if not a plumber's snake.

Yes, this could be messy. Forgive us. Help us forgive each other.

MIKE MULLIGAN
AND HIS MARY ANNE

God, she's devastated. Virtually every expert thing she knows is now deemed obsolete, no longer needed. And she's been working so hard to prove herself—*I can still perform; I still have value here*—that she hasn't upgraded the program.

"I've dug myself into a hole. Let's face it: They think I'm a rusty old relic, and, well, maybe I am."

Her pain tears me and sends me to the bookshelf to find one of my favorite redemption stories: *Mike Mulligan and His Steam Shovel*. Mary Anne, the steam shovel, is named for a woman and loved like a red Camaro that will never grow old. But of course "she" does.

And when Mary Anne becomes obsolete and has carelessly dug herself into a cellar that she cannot drive out of, Mike Mulligan remains faithful. Her friends help her become resourceful. Mary Anne survives, her boiler converted to a furnace, warming the town hall in Popperville. Anyville.

OK, it's just a story. OK, even implausible. But Lord, please use this fiction—and this prayer—to give her hope for a future. Help her—and me, as I age—always to find a place of usefulness. With a little help from our friends. With you remaining faithful as Mike Mulligan was to his beloved Mary Anne.

MOTHER: A PEACEFUL PARTING

She's spending this day waiting with her mother, waiting for death to slip in and clip the cord. God, I'm not sure either of them is ready for the moment, the leave-taking that will separate daughter from mother more dramatically than did birth.

As a birthing woman waits, not knowing the exact time of delivery, allow this daughter grace to stand by, hold on, and be ready for the hour.

As a birthing woman gives her baby permission to leave her womb, allow this daughter grace to give her mother leave of this world. So as to meet you in another. At the end of the tunnel, welcomed with open arms.

THE LINES ARE DOWN

Discard not an old friend, for the new one cannot equal him.

ECCLESIASTICUS 9:10, NAB

God, we used to be such pals, and then I got cut off.

Phone calls not returned. Get-togethers foreshortened. Laughter forced. "Have I done something to offend you?"

No. She's just busy, very busy. Always on the run. Always out to lunch.

I give up. The lines are down. The connection's broken.

Whatever it's really about, I haven't a clue, but this rejection hurts. It just hurts.

God, be my balm (not my bomb).

Be with her. Be for her.

Wherever she goes.

CHRISTMAS CHEER

She says she doesn't want to put up Christmas decorations this year. Can't. Won't. "I did it for the kids. They're gone. They have trees of their own. Who needs it?"

I coax, urge. Maybe not a tree. That's a lot of work. But some ornaments, some lights?

"I'm tired. Don't push it. Got to get some sleep. Good night."

God, I understand "tired" when it means depressed. What shall we do, you and I?

OK. I'll buy her a tall, fat, white candle. One candle. And suggest that she light it every night while eating. All through Advent. In hope. For hope.

And you? If I provide the candle, will you provide the spark? Of hope. For love.

With cheer.

FEELING SAFE

God, the older I get the more I sense that I feel loved when I feel safe. I'm not sure the two feelings *should* be equated; I'm just telling you what I've learned about myself. And apparently I'm not the first to think this. George Eliot wrote: "Friendship is the inexpressible comfort of feeling safe with a person." Is there a universal pull, tugging us back toward the womb?

And with this friend of so many years, well, I feel loved, which is to say I feel safe. When I'm in her kitchen. When she's in my backyard. When we're on the phone. And the safety I feel in her presence or at the sound of her voice enables me to leave her presence feeling stronger, more secure, more ready to step into a world that doesn't always feel safe.

Thank you, Lord, for this time-tested friend, who has proven herself as a refuge and refreshment.

SISTERS *and* ME

OF COURSE, I REMEMBER!

God, she said my bathroom curtains, fashioned by my very own hands from white bath towels ... she said they looked like tampons. I didn't think she was looking for a moment of shared laughter. She just blurted it out, straight-faced. With a hint of disgust?

I pretended she hadn't said it. I pretended I hadn't been hurt.

But the comment lingered in the back of my mind. Ten years? Twelve? I've moved away since then. I have a new bathroom. I have new lacy curtains.

Yet the old ones, perfectly deconstructed, remain as towels, hanging in the shower. This morning I wrapped my wet hair in one of those white wonders, and I thought of her tactless remark. God, such a petty memory is pathetic. Forgive me, as I forgive her.

Next time I think of the tampon towels, I will lighten up the story. (She did have a way with words. What a simile.) And let it bring a smile.

MAKING FRIENDS USED TO BE EASIER

When the generous time of youth has wholly passed, it becomes hard to make new connections.... In youth the heart is responsive and ready to be generous, and the hand aches for the grasp of a comrade's hand.

HUGH BLACK, *Friendship*

God, it *was* easier to make friends when I was younger. To make connections now—there's so much to explain, and yes, maybe the deficiency is "generosity." After a certain age, how many of us are generous enough to listen through … to trust in … to tarry with … until the passing acquaintance is a fast friend?

God, the old friends are comfortable and steady. But maybe it's time for a stretch. Restore unto me the responsiveness of youth, well, at least a bit of it. Help me to reach out. Open a hand. Let a comrade in.

MY TURN FOR SURGERY

Now it's my turn. Surgery in the major degree. Thank you, that everything came out OK. No complications, though the pain—ye-ow.

When she heard I would be alone all day, she said she'd come, sit through the surgery (as if it were a wake?), and stay till dinnertime. She ignored my insincere protests and was there—and more present than I realized.

The day after "the procedure," the woman in the next bed asked about "the woman." Who was she?

A girlfriend.

"You're so lucky." And then she told me what I hardly remembered: My friend had sat at my side, reading a book and holding my hand all day.

Thank you for this silent gift. Someone to see me through. Show me ways to repay the kindness.

SISTERS *and* ME

ALICE DOESN'T LIVE HERE, DOES SHE?

She's selling her parents' place, and it's tearing her apart. It's more than a house. It's the roof she was raised under, the rooms she rattled in, the sidewalk she pedaled over, the stoop she kissed on. It feels as if she's putting her childhood up for sale, the whole lot of it, when she'd rather be building a shrine that would mark for perpetuity her land of play and puberty. She hasn't lived there for decades, and yet she grieves as if the loss were new.

I can understand this—the times I've wanted to hold on to something, someone, someplace that has already let me leave. I thought we'd made our peace—this person, place, or thing and I—and then, wham, the calm

is broken by a wave of grief set in motion by ... usually something less dramatic than a house-closing.

God, this letting go stuff. It's never going to stop, is it? A person here, a place there, and then a prized possession, until it's my time to go for good? So, for my friend and for myself, I ask for yet more grace to say good-bye to all those roofs and all those rooms and all they hold—or did.

CANCER CALL

God, by your grace she licked the cancer the first time. But it's back. And if the disease doesn't kill her, the treatments might.

I went by yesterday to visit, and we just sat there and cried. She, for pain, in despair. I, for her, in hope.

Let my hope be counted as hers.

Lord, I can't see this as being a time for a prayer of relinquishment. This is time for fight songs and battle cries. Disease and death should not take this round. She's too young. I beg you—bind the horse and rider, and drown them in the sea. Restore her health and grant her life.

Let my prayer be counted as heard.

RESTORE UNTO HER ...

Her child—her bundle of joy—has grown up to become her sorrow and shame. Broken her heart. Forsaken her ways. Worried her sick.

Her friends used to ask about her son—fine, thank you—but now they've given it up, not wanting to see her eyes drown in disappointment.

God, your Word hints that your chosen Mary knew the pain of dashed hopes for her son. And yet she loved him, loved him still. May that kind of mother-love draw my friend's son back to her—and ultimately back to you, the God who is love, the God who is redcemer, the God who waits with hope.

SISTERS *and* ME

WISHING WELL

There is no friend like an old friend
Who has shared our morning days.

OLIVER WENDELL HOLMES

Recently my dreams have been peopled with childhood friends who are now strangers to me. My night imagination spans the gap in our acquaintance and we're all grown-ups, still familiar, working together, wishing together, all one and well.

And I wish them well. God, wherever they are, I pray that you would make your presence obvious to them. Plant yourself in their lives (or maybe their dreams) and walk with them—even play with them—throughout these dusky days.

PRAYERS *for*

IN GOOD COMPANY

God, her hair is as gray as an old snowbank and yet she's never lived alone. Parents. Roommates. Husband. Children. But then the husband walked, and now the last child is heading to college. And I can hear panic in her voice. *Got to find me a man. Find me. Find him. Quick.*

God, I pray you would bring such a one into her world, but only if he's a good man and only if he would be good for her.

Until then, calm her spirit. (The panic doesn't become her.) Put her at ease with herself. Assure her that her house is indeed a home, even if she's living alone but for you.

BEFORE I LEAVE, I'D SAY PLEASE ...

A study exercise posed the scenario: Suppose you knew you had twenty-four hours to live. List and prioritize your "must do's."

My short list called for phone conversations with all my siblings—the sisters who anticipated my birth, poked at my belly, shared my closet, taught me to ride.

We've never let one another hide. So if I were so drastically exiting the scene, I would say hello and make a few requests:

"Please forgive me any offense—what I have done or neglected to do.

"Please do not forget me today, tomorrow, or in the stretch ahead.

"Please tell me you love me, as I love you.

"Please hold me close as I see this through."

Lord, if I knew I had twenty-four hours left on this earth, I would make the same requests of you. And here make this prayer even today, though I expect no departure anytime soon.

I LAUGH, SHE LAUGHS, WE LAUGH

God, we laugh together more than we did ten years ago. Is it a change in her? A change in me? Probably in both of us, as you have chiseled away some of our sharp edges. For this I thank you. And with this prayer, I shall call her up and, yes, laugh. You'll join us?

SISTERS *and* ME

REMEMBER TO FORGET

My friend exclaimed, "I am like Lot's wife. My life is petrified because I keep looking back."

PAUL TOURNIER, *The Person Reborn*

God, she's haunted by the trespass that to her defines her past. She says she knows you've forgiven her, but that doesn't mean she can forgive herself.

I think of your curious words in Luke 17:32, "Remember Lot's wife!" You give a command to remember the past. But that command is intrinsically an admonition to let it go. *Remember the fate of the woman who could not walk straight away from the fire.*

God, if she needs to make amends, give her the courage to do so. Then give her the freedom to *learn* from the past without letting it lure her back or paralyze her stride.

AU REVOIR L'EMPLOYMENT

She's retiring today—feeling as much ambivalence as she felt the day she graduated from college.

They call graduation a commencement, but who are they kidding? It's a day marking endings as much as beginnings: saying good-bye to a daily routine, a colleague camaraderie, a sequence of goals, a self-definition.

And here she is again, facing similar losses. This time the transition isn't given a positive, hopeful appellation. *Retirement*. The word says the best has been, though everyone nervously assures her it's yet to be.

God, help her sort through the loss and the potential gain. She now holds a new gift in her hands: No, not the gold watch but the time it measures. The gift of hours. Allow her to appreciate it and its worth, to use it wisely and well, to enjoy it to the end of her earthly days.

Bless her on this day: her commencement.

GRAVESIDE VISIT, AFTER THE FUNERAL

God, she's gone, and I want to tell you how much I will miss her. She was good to me and for me.

How much I will miss "us"—who she and I were when we were together. Safe and secure from all alarm. Or so it seemed until now, when the *we* is reduced to me, standing here alone while she lies silent in this grave.

God, our relationship is buried here with her. Yes, our times together remain in my memory. But they're memories—forged and mounted, finished, like the bronze angel statues at the gates of this cemetery. Time will only wear the treasures thin, not add any new precious layers.

So let me say it again, in case you didn't hear me. I will miss her. I will miss "us."

I'm sorry she is gone.

ANNIVERSARY COMMEMORATION

It's their anniversary. A shiny, precious one. Time to celebrate longevity and fidelity. Do I sense a pride in their accomplishment? *What do you know? We made it!*

She and he—they've been together more years than they've been apart. Happy? Not deliriously. But they still sometimes whisper in church. And after the service, walking toward the car, they still reach for each other. It is enough.

God, thank you for the life they have shared together: what she has given him, what he has given her. As they remember, fuel their affection and commitment. Oh, go ahead, while you're at it, ignite their passion. Lord, let it burn.

SISTERS *and* ME

A DISCONTENTED JOURNEY

She's got exactly what she thought she wanted and, no, it's suddenly not. She mourns the spring, worries the winter. She misses the lean years, wishes for green years, and can't see the current splendor of bloom, marvelous bloom.

OK. She's not the only guilty party. I think the scenario may be the fate of woman, living perpetually in her discontented season for any number of reasons: the man she has, the man she lost; the job she landed, the job she could have had; the body she was born with, the body childbirth left behind....

Lord, remind us of your truth: "Now is the time of God's favor, now is the day of salvation" (2 Cor 6:2). Remind us to sing a summer song even if we're convinced we're in a winter land.

BIG MAN AROUND THE HOUSE

God, she says she never had imagined it would be like this—her husband's retirement. He thinks he's being helpful, telling her how to run the house, as if it were suddenly his domain. For fifty years he hasn't given a rip about vacuuming wall to wall. This is unfortunate, yes, but now he's become the expert on efficient motion and maximized strokes.

Not that he offers to take on the task. No. He just demonstrates the technique, so she'll have a better handle on it next week.

And the kitchen—he sees a better way to arrange the cupboards, cut the bagels, load the dishwasher. Not that he actually puts the dishes in the dishwasher.

Give her—give *them*—wisdom and patience. May she welcome and make room for a new teammate. May he learn what it means to play on the home team. Draw them both out of the house, widen their worlds, so he doesn't suffocate her, so she doesn't strangle him.

SAME FRIEND

Some people have a rare gift.... The ability to treat sick people as if they were truly themselves.

EDNA MCCANN, *The Heritage Book, 1985*

God, since her accident—burns, horrible burns—she won't leave the house except to go to the doctor. She doesn't want anyone to stare at her, or maybe the stares are preferable to the people who get a glimpse and then turn away.

I go and visit, sometimes not convinced she wants even me to see what she's lost, who she's become, as if the body were the all of it.

Maybe I should write this prayer for her, for courage and perspective. But I write it for me, that I will treat her not as a cracked pot but as my dear friend, maybe fragile and frayed, but tried and true. Friend. Amen.

GRAYING GARDENER: A VISIT

Last evening I stood and watched her plant her garden. Like a girl on a dirt pile, she dug valleys, made them rivers; built mountains, pushed them flat. With those mud-moving hands she set a year in motion: burying seeds to harvest a bushel of life. She's done this so often, two score and more springs, in faith that she'll pick the fruit in its season. God, grant her an eternity of summers, sunshine to ripen the fruit of her spirit.

BEYOND MY REACH

Every year my Christmas card list gets shorter—one friend, then a few, then more "passing on" beyond the reach of the postal service.

Someday, what if I'm the only one left? What if every line in my book is crossed out? What if every address book that includes my name is thrown out?

Lord, I don't want to stay here that long. Not today, but soon, I'd be just as happy if you invited me to a reunion with my circle of friends. I'm getting tired and am ready for a change of pace—maybe a party with the heavenly host?

AN ENCOURAGING WORD

Instead of a gem or a flower, cast the gift of a lovely thought into the heart of a friend.

GEORGE MACDONALD

Lord, let me be like a flower girl casting petals in the procession—dropping encouraging words in the conversation to enhance the celebration.

TOPICAL INDEX